A horse for Pansy

PAGC Third Level Services

A horse for Pansy

Edward Mirasty, Ed PhD(c) and Vince Brittain Ed.D(c)

Copyright 2023 Prince Albert Grand Council. All rights reserved.

Published by:
Big Moose Publishing
Box 127 Site 601 RR#6
Saskatoon, SK S7K 3J9
www.bigmoosepublishing.com

ISBN: 978-1-989840-59-7
Big Moose Publishing 06/2023

DEDICATION

From Left to Right: Leonard (Red) Mirasty, Bertha Mirasty, Alphonse McCallum, Rose (Mirasty) McCallum, Pansy Mirasty, and Kookum Mary Ayasiw (front middle)

This story is dedicated to past victims of Indian Residential Schools found buried in unmarked graves around Indian Residential Schools.

This book is also dedicated to my (Edward Mirasty) mother, Bertha (Mirasty) Beatty, who passed away in 2011, at age 65. She shared her story as part of the Truth and Reconciliation where she attended the All Saints Indian Residential School in Prince Albert, Saskatchewan. Her sister Pansy, died at age 9 while attending the Indian Residential School.

MISSION STATEMENT

The Prince Albert Grand Council Executive will provide leadership in a comprehensive way to address issues of common concern that affect PAGC First Nation communities and its members, including Treaty protection, resource development and revenue sharing.

(PAGC Chief's Strategic Plan, 2021, p. 3).

Grand Chief Brian Hardlotte, member of Lac La Ronge Indian Band, was elected in October 2017 and is serving his 2nd term as Grand Chief.

Vice Chief Joseph Tsannie, member of the Hatchet Lake Denesuline First Nation; was re-elected in October 2015 and is serving his 3rd term as Vice Chief.

Vice Chief Christopher Jobb, member of Peter Ballantyne Cree Nation; was elected in October 2016 and is serving his 2nd term as Vice Chief.

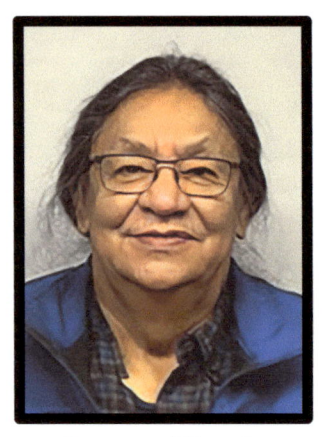

George Mirasty

"It's part of the healing process…"

The Truth and Reconciliation Commission is a national undertaking to acknowledge and share the unpleasant realities of our residential school history. One of its goals is to "promote awareness and public education of Canadians about the IRS system and its impacts."

- George Mirasty (former Indian Residential School Survivor

Indigenizing is "emphasizing holistic education over compartmentalized subjects, engaging talking circles, and using traditional arts, crafts, activities, and land-based learning to explore curriculum.[1]"

[1] Morcom, L., Freeman, K. (2018). Niinwi - kiinwa - kiinwi: Building non-indigenous allies in education through indigenous pedagogy. Canadian Society for the Study of Education: Canadian Journal of Education; 41 (3), pp 820

ABOUT the AUTHORS

My name is **Edward Mirasty** (Lac LaRonge Indian Band Member), and I am the Director of Education for the Prince Albert Grand Council. I have been happily married for over thirty-one years, and we now have a little girl named Lilly-B. I am in my final year of an Interdisciplinary Ph.D. Program at the University of Saskatchewan. I have been involved in education for over twenty-eight years, most of it in administration. Our education office has evolved over the past three years to develop more resources to share the rich history, culture, and languages of our PAGC members.

Edward Mirasty

Vince Brittain is a James Smith Cree Nation Band member who grew up and attended school at Bernard Constant Community School. He has been married to his wife Connie for over twenty-one years. They have two boys. The eldest, Merit, has completed his second year at the University of Regina in Social Work, and has now entered his first year of Education through the First Nations University of Canada. His youngest, Merik, is attending Grade 12 at Carlton Comprehensive High School. Vince has been involved in education for over 26 years and is currently finishing up his first year of a Doctorate of Education through the University of Saskatchewan. He currently works at the Prince Albert Grand Council as their Third Level Specialist. He believes in honesty, integrity, and trustworthiness, which leads to strong relationships. Vince's parents truly believed in education and strongly supported him in his educational journey. They would be proud of him as he continues with his educational journey and helps empower communities as they move forward.

Vince Brittain

While visiting my relatives who spoke in both Cree and English, I listened attentively as my uncle and auntie shared their story of their late sister, named Pansy.

Pansy

Similar to her sisters named Rose and Violet, she was also named after a flower, Pansy.

Like many other First Nations children, she was taken to an Indian Residential School in Prince Albert.

All Saints Indian Residential School (Prince Albert)

While she attended the All Saints Indian Residential School, she began to feel sick.

PA dormitories – barracks, ca. 1949, ACC Gen Synod Bernice Logan fonds/P2004-09

Girls in front of hut, ca. 1950, ACC Bernice Logan fonds/P2004-09-136

When she complained about her increased stomach pains, she would be forced to go to the infirmary or be assigned domestic work duties.

My mom shared that sometimes the nurse and other caregivers would force her to clean the floors with a toothbrush when she complained about her pain.

She would also add that the caregivers would sometimes draw a circle around her little sister, and have the children laugh and make fun of her. My mom felt helpless, all she could do was watch and cry.

Soon after returning home, Pansy was brought back to Prince Albert's Holy Family Hospital where she was diagnosed with leukemia.

I had to swallow my tears as my auntie and uncle continued their last few memories of Pansy. They would add that during her last evening in the hospital, she asked my uncle for one last wish.

She asked that if she got better, she'd like to return to the reserve and ride my uncle's horse along the fields.

My auntie Violet's heart ached as she shared how she still remembers holding her little sister's weak, and small hands.

She would pass away the next day.

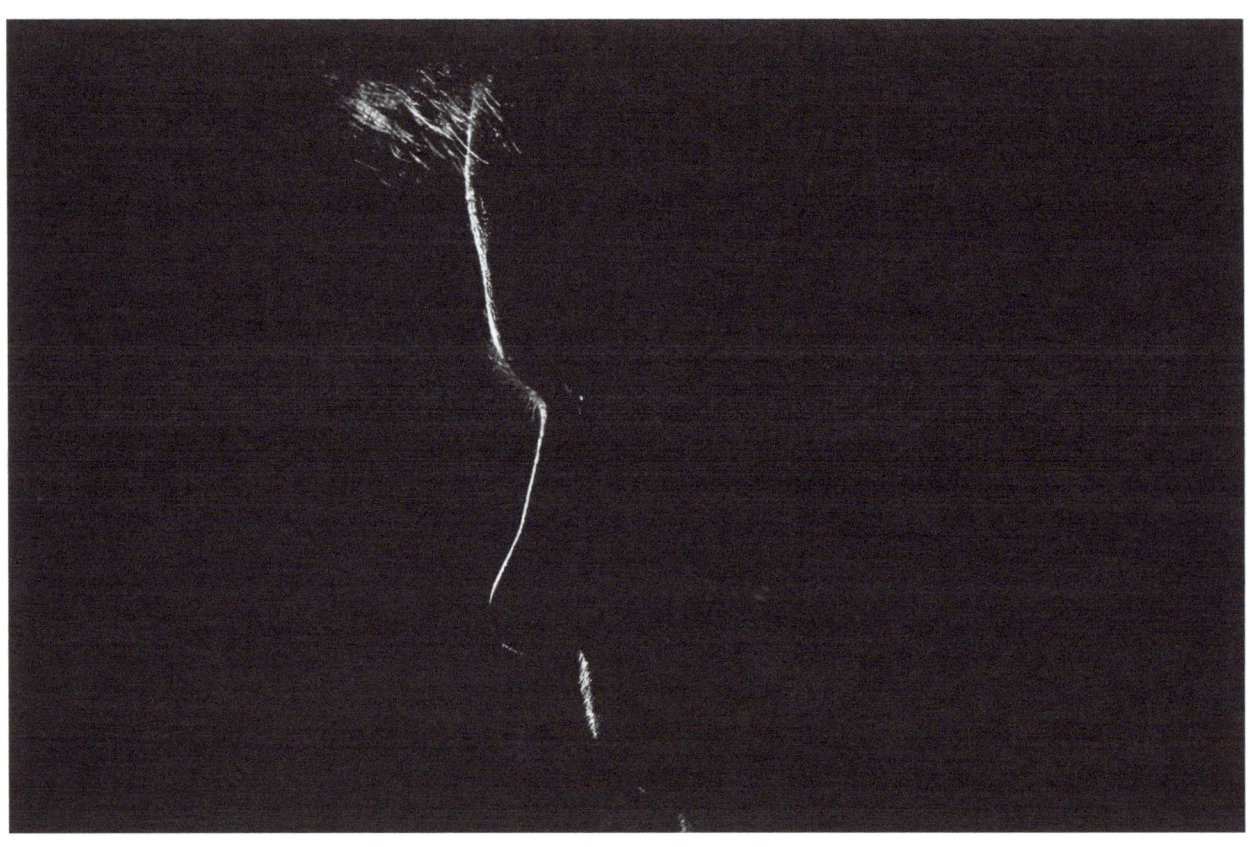

Although it was difficult to hear my uncle and auntie share their memory of their little sister, Pansy, understanding the history of Residential School and the intergenerational impacts it would have on survivors, helps the younger generation to remember, and for everyone to begin their journey of healing.

Girl in photo: Lilly B Mirasty

Lilly B was named after her late great grandmother (Bertha) who shared the story of her late sister, Pansy. LillyB represents the resiliency of cultural, political, and societal change of future indigenous youth.

BIBLIOGRAPHY

Prince Albert Daily Herald. (2018). If you don't have forgiveness in your heart, it's going to become a stone. Retrieved on July 15th, 2022 from https://paherald.sk.ca/if-you-dont-have- forgiveness-in-your-heart-its-going-to-become-a-stone/

Lakowski, C. (2014). Local residential school artifacts to end up in national art project. Retrieved on November 10th, 2021 from https://www2.uregina.ca/education/saskindianresidentialschools/wp-content/uploads/2017/11/Local-residential-school-artifacts-to-end-up-in-national-art-project-_-paNOW.pdf.

Mirasty, V., H. (2020, October 29th). Personal story-telling session.

The University of Regina. (2022). Shattering the silence: The Hidden History of Indian Residential Schools in Saskatchewan ebook. Project of Heart ebook. Retrieved on July 15th, 2022 from https://www2.uregina.ca/education/saskindianresidentialschools/st-albans-indian-residential- school/

www.ingramcontent.com/pod-product-compliance
Lightning Source LLC
Chambersburg PA
CBHW050848010526
44107CB00017BA/1220